D1560547

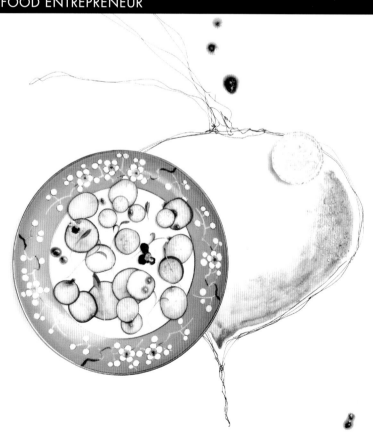

WHERE WOMEN CREATE BUSINESS:

# THE ARTISAN FOOD ENTREPRENEUR

## PROFILES IN PASSION AND SUCCESS

BY JO PACKHAM

# PRESS

215 Historic 25th Street, Ogden, Utah

© 2014 Jo Packham

First published in the United States of America in 2014 by
Quarry Books, a member of
Quayside Publishing Group
100 Cummings Center
Suite 406-L
Beverly, Massachusetts 01915-6101
Telephone: (978) 282-9590
Fax: (978) 283-2742
www.quarrybooks.com

10 9 8 7 6 5 4 3 2 1

ISBN: 978-1-59253-894-2

*Production Manager:* **Brandy Shay**

*Copy Editor:* **Amber Demien**

*Contributing Editor:* **Sandra Evertson**

*Cover Designer:* **Sandra Salamony**

*Book Designer:* **Matt Shay**

*Production Artist:* **Chelsi Johnston**

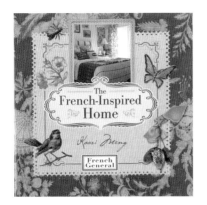
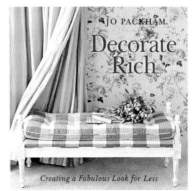

Like anything, being an author is demanding, tedious, frustrating, lonely, and anonymous … yet at the end of the day it is exhilarating, satisfying, rewarding, and profitable.

There is no feeling that I know of that is equal to going into a bookstore and seeing your book on the shelves. And if it just happens to be among the "Employees' Picks" or on the shelf with the "Top 10 Best Sellers" … you just simply may never have a better day!

Have you ever thought about how the success of a book is judged? Is it by the sheer numbers of books sold? Is it by the reviews received or the awards earned? Is it by the money that is made? Or is it by the respect that is acquired from those who know you well or not at all?

I was in publishing for years and had sold, quite literally, millions of books, and every single morning my cute little mother would call and ask me if I had to go to work that day, couldn't I stay home? What was so important for me to accomplish when I got there? She just could not quite grasp the concept that her daughter was a publisher. After all, publishers lived in New York City and wrote fiction or biographies.

Then one day she called and there was an excitement in her voice I had not heard before. She said to me, "You have really made it, haven't you?" I asked what made her think that today I could consider myself a success, and she said, "I saw your books in the library today and I was so proud." That day was the one day in my publishing career that I shall never forget and that no other day or recognition of success will ever surpass.

I hope in your career that you know the joy, experience the rewards, and share the success of a "best seller" with someone you love!

My best always
Jo

# JO PACKHAM

I am in my 60s, I have been an entrepreneur for 35 years, and I have worked in publishing my entire adult career. It was not a childhood dream, a focus for college studies, or part of a five-year business plan ... it just simply happened one day with a really good idea.

In the early '80s my husband graduated from law school in California, and we moved back to our hometown of Ogden, Utah, to open his law practice and to begin my new first dream: I opened a small retail store with my best friend called Apple Arts, where we sold art supplies to the college students and local crafters. We ran a good business and worked hard, but the income in a small town with an even smaller art supply store was negligible.

One day at a craft show, while shopping for new inventory for the store, I discovered a series of simple and basic counted cross-stitch books; we ordered them without a second thought. They sold like they were printed on gold paper ... there was something in this new handmade craft that was worth investigating.

Inspired by their author, fascinated by cross-stitch, and ready for a new more profitable venture, Linda and I sold the store. I found a new partner (which is a story for another time) and we began the learning curve of designing, publishing, and selling soft-cover, staple-bound, 24-page, cross-stitch pattern books for $4.95. In those days I

graphed, stitched, and wrote instructions for our first four cross-stitch books at my kitchen table.

As with any successful new venture your product must be different or better than your competitor, so our books contained designs that were more sophisticated and offered more than just cross-stitch designs; we included pages of full-color photography, patterns, and techniques for teaching the new cross-stitch enthusiast how to take her finished cross-stitch pieces and use them as the fabric to make pillows, quilts, clothing, and more. Even then I loved to tell the whole story, and whenever possible we added food or shot the stitched pieces in the kitchen – where else but the heart of the home?

Millions of cross-stitch books were published and sold in the next six or seven years, and then the bottom fell out of the cross-stitch market ... as it will with any market. So, needing a job, I proposed our becoming a "packager" of how-to books to major publishers (which is also a story for another day), and we began publishing books in all categories of handmade with Oxmoor House and Meredith.

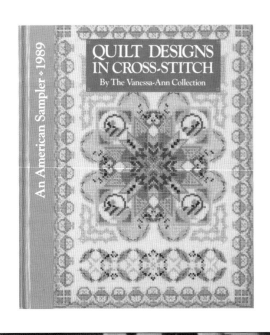

An American Sampler ◆ 1989

QUILT DESIGNS
IN CROSS-STITCH
By The Vanessa-Ann Collection

Vanessa-Ann's
Holidays In
Cross-Stitch
1992

That was 35 years ago and in the years since I have published thousands of books that have sold millions of copies. I have worked with authors from around the world on subjects from antique cross-stitch samplers, to master woodworking, to baking pies … and I am still at my kitchen table.

Over the years I have watched the industry change and create an entirely new business model. Authors, books, and publishing no longer have the same strategies or expected outcomes and incomes.

When I began with my first hardbound book on counted cross-stitch designs with Meredith Publishing, you could calculate that if you sold 10,000 books you knew you would be paid a royalty of approximately 50 cents to $1 per book, so your check would equal $5,000 to $10,000. The books were sold to independent retailers at a 50 percent discount off of retail and the retailers paid the invoices within 30 days.

In the early 1980s, with the rise of the big-box chain stores, the buying and selling of books began to change. Big-box buying power demanded higher discounts, delayed invoicing and the right to return, which meant lower and delayed royalties for authors. And over the years the consumer has demanded books have more pages, contain more recipes, projects, and information for a lower price … again all affecting the royalties earned by the authors.

## Fluffy Peanut Butter Frosting

*about 2 cups  Prep Time: 10 minutes*

1 jar (7oz.) marshmallow cream
½ cup Skippy® Creamy Peanut Butter
½ cup margarine
1¾ cups confectioners sugar
2 Tbsp. milk
½ tsp. vanilla extract

**1.** In small bowl, with electric mixer on low speed, beat marshmallow cream, Skippy® Creamy Peanut Butter and margarine until smooth.
**2.** Increase speed to medium and beat in remaining ingredients until blended.

**Serving Suggestion** Use to frost cupcakes or your favorite chocolate cake.

101  Desserts & More

Toasted Monkey Sandwiches

29

## Royal Cheesecake

**12-14 servings**

1½ cups graham cracker crumbs
2 Tbsp. granulated sugar
¼ cup butter, melted
2 packages (8 oz. each) cream cheese
4 cups milk
½ tsp. ground cinnamon
2 packages lemon instant pudding mix
1 jar (10 oz.) Welch's® Grape Jam

1. Preheat oven to 350°F.
2. In a bowl, combine graham cracker crumbs and sugar. Add melted butter; stir thoroughly to blend.
3. Pack mixture firmly into bottom, and about two-thirds up sides of a 9-inch spring-form pan.
4. Bake until lightly browned. Cool.
5. In a bowl, beat cream cheese until softened.
6. Add 1 cup milk, a little at a time, blending until mixture is smooth.
7. Add remaining milk, cinnamon, and pudding mix. Beat until well blended with an electric mixer.
8. Pour into crust and chill until set, about 2 hours.
9. Just before serving, spread jar of Welch's® Grape Jam over surface of cheesecake.

Uncle Sam's Favorite **Welch's** *The National Drink*

page 106

In those early years a how-to designer who authored a series of respectable-selling books could brag of making a good living that would send her children to college. Today, in our category of how-to there is a very different ending. Unless you are a phenomenon and best-selling author such as Ree Drummond, an icon such as Martha Stewart, or you just "hit" with an idea for a book on a trend that is beginning to explode, like *Decorating Junk Market Style* (JunkMarket Girls, 2005) by Ki Nassauer, the story of authors and their royalties ends quite differently.

everything
goes with
ice cream
by Koralee Teichroob

111 Decadent Treats from
Raspberry Sorbet to Cream Cookie Pie
plus Fabulous Handmade Party Ideas

Today, I have my own publishing imprint, WWC PRESS, that publishes with Quarry Books, and we create not only how-to books but also cookbooks and business books for the artisan woman entrepreneur. Today I tell anyone who wants to write a book that if you are creating it for the money, I would suggest that you invest your time where the financial return could be more substantial. If you want to author a book to help you sell a product, to support an established brand, or because the subject of the book is something you do every day, making a book a second source of income and exposure for what exists, then authoring a book is probably a good idea.

For example: If you are a really good cook and you have always dreamed of writing your own cookbook, the process is time-consuming and expensive. There is the buying of the ingredients, the testing of the recipes, the photography, and the proofing of it all. If you own a restaurant or author a successful food blog and you cook every day, then it is a different scenario entirely. You only need to pay for a photographer … and bloggers are usually their own professional food photographers. With this narrative you are working smarter by reselling what you have already sold once — promoting a restaurant, blog, or brand — and you are expanding your community through a new medium. This is truly working smarter and not harder.

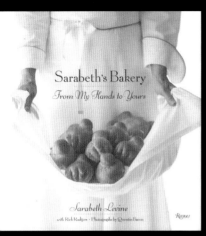

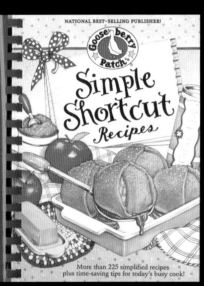

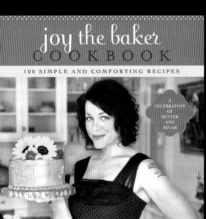

My advice for a foodie who still believes that she wants to write a book is to create a short and concise proposal, of no more than one page, that contains: a working title; a table of contents; a "short" press release indicating who you are, what you have accomplished, and your credentials for authoring and promoting a book; and six recipes and six photographs of the finished dishes made from those recipes. You should also include a short paragraph listing the three top-selling books on the market that would be considered competitors to your title, and why one more book on this subject should be published. What makes your approach different from those already in the bookstores?

I would then go to the bookstore and find those publishers who publish books similar to the one you are proposing. Publishers are very different – one may publish inexpensive $9.95 cookbooks with little photography, while others produce beautiful, collectable cookbooks with price tags of $40 plus. Buy the cookbooks, study them, call the publisher and see if the editor who worked on the book is still working there or who took her place, and ask for her email address. Some publishers do not accept unsolicited manuscripts, but some do. If they do not accept unsolicited manuscripts, ask them their procedure to be followed in order to submit.

If you have a successful blog it is always easier and the step above can be eliminated because editors scan blogs looking for the most popular, and it is often these women who get book deals.

Email your proposal with a very short cover letter to all of those publishers that fit your criteria. Do not send your book to one publisher, wait for a reply, and then send it to another; send it to everyone at the same time. See who is interested, who is offering the best terms in their contract, and with which editor you feel you have the best rapport.

Be prepared to not only produce the book but also to actively promote and sell it. Publishers today are as interested in you and your selling/promotional abilities and connections as they are in your subject matter. A very famous person can sell a substantial number of a not-so-good book, but it is very difficult for an unknown, first-time author to sell very many copies of even a brilliant book.

And, I must tell you, across the decades and through all of the innumerable ups and downs, and very hard work … I still love this job and I am still at my kitchen table.

I am inspired by the packaging of books for the most talented of authors, the writing of my own books, and the compiling of books that include many of us. After all, if there are 40 women in a book, promoting the book and each other, the chances of it being a success are far better than if someone is doing everything all by themselves ... and the book signings and the promotional parties are just more fun!

Remember, only you can create the dream.

END

# LUCY BENJAMIN

Lucy Benjamin is originally from Central London and is now living in what she calls Central East Blue Hill. Lucy had never tasted granola until nine years ago when she and her family moved to Down East, Maine. She first tasted granola at a local farmers' market, but when her favorite baker stopped selling it, she started making her own and varying the recipes for fun. When Lucy forgot to make a cake for the village bake sale, she raided the huge pickle jar of granola she had made for her husband and, amazingly, her business began!

It's been a wonderful few years! In London, I had a good career as a chartered surveyor (a commercial real estate professional). In 2004, my husband and I moved to Maine with our two little girls. Soon after we had another baby and began to restore our old family cottage, the recession hit. My husband, an architect, had little work, so I started a property management business to bring in architectural work. A few years later, my granola business started and took off as demand for the product simply grew.

I began the business at the farmers' market, the local co-op, and a few other nearby shops and markets. I met Abby Freethy from North Woods Gourmet Girl at a local food sampling festival, and we started doing shows together. Compatible, but not competitive, Abby and I have a great time — Maine women working together! Recently we went to San Francisco for the Fancy Food Show, which was a great experience and a chance to make inroads into new and different markets.

My business is growing nicely thanks to our developing online business, increasing publicity in blogs and in the press, and our wonderful Maine farmers' market customers who spread the word. In February, my granola made it to the dining section of the *New York Times* — it was a real thrill to be called "über-artisanal" by the *Times*! We now sell in over 80 shops and the number is increasing all the time.

I love being in business and having the ability to create jobs and to manufacture a real, high-quality product. When I listen to the monthly job figures, it is wonderful to know that I am even a small part of growing the larger economy. It is also important to me to be in the healthy food business, and I believe it is particularly important to market and maintain a product that is both healthy and affordable. At the same time, I hope to have a broader appeal to the gourmet market as a whole. I have recently shifted my focus to year-round, non-seasonal gourmet and high-quality small chains and markets.

There are, of course, challenges that come along with starting and developing your own business. The clichéd challenge of "juggling" comes quickly to mind — juggling time, delegating responsibilities, and balancing the origins of the business with the changes that come with growth. Every day there is so much to do — updating websites, preparing for shows, monitoring quality, managing employees ("granola elves"), making donations, completing applications, invoicing, paying bills, purchasing specialty ingredients, making packaging decisions — zillions of tasks that every small business has to attend to.

# 5 Points on
# How to Work with Your Husband:

1. Strengths: Work out what his strengths are and use them. My husband is very organized and detail oriented. I encourage him to use those traits where they are important. He keeps the inventory of supplies, organizes the stock, does packaging, etc.

2. Common Interests: Our interests are so aligned that we can bounce ideas off each other. He understands the business details. He sees the problems and knows what to do.

3. Team Work: We have reversed roles in many ways. I am much more focused on the business, and he takes care of the house; this allows me to concentrate on my work. My husband is happy to stay home whilst I go off to do sales/markets/shows etc. It would be really hard if we were both traveling all the time.

4. Communication: Communicating about time is essential. I understand what he is doing on any given day/week (tending animals, house, architectural work, garden) so I know how much I have to manage with everything else (children, business, meals, etc.). We have a wonderful blackboard with a grid that lists all appointments/activities/events for everyone so we know at a glance where everyone has to be.

5. Be Supportive: Clifton has always believed in the business more than I have and this is totally supportive. I couldn't imagine not having this kind of emotional backing, it makes all the difficult bits so much easier. Clifton is really patient with the granola elves; when things go wrong, he will explain over and over when something needs to be done differently, which is not necessarily my style.

Needless to say, there are disappointments from time to time. Recently, I delegated an application for a great organic fair to my husband without giving him enough information about all the organic and local ingredients we were to use. I assumed Clifton knew but I assumed too much, and we were rejected from the fair. This was extremely frustrating and painful, but I was unclear with my instructions, and my husband made a totally genuine mistake. Of course, as with any rejection in business, it's hard not to take it personally, but it is important to learn how to move on, and I'm trying. Being in business with your husband can be especially challenging at times. It's great when all goes well, but very hard at other times. Overall, though, he is clever and calm, especially in a crisis or a crunch, and I am very lucky!

I am very excited about our latest product — toffee bars! My friend, Neil Reiter, had the wonderful idea of a granola-coated, chocolate, toffee bar finished with delicious sea salt. The toffee bars give our business new impetus and energy, and I can see Lucy's Granola expanding to other products and markets. Neil is helping push us to new stages and I expect he will become part of the business moving forward.

Overall, I love being in the food business, having a business, and being able to incorporate family life into the work day when needed. I think I am the luckiest person I know.

END

# KELLI BESS

Slide Ridge Winery/Slide Ridge Honey in Mendon, Utah, is a family-run business with a long-standing tradition of beekeeping, which is the foundation of their all-natural products. They even raise their own queen bees, practicing sustainable beekeeping methods that work with the lifecycle of the bees. Maintaining strong hives results in healthy bees, which in turn produces an elite-quality honey straight from the bee to the bottle … to you!

We are a family operation, all taking part in a dream that my brother, Martin James, had of building a business around sustainable agriculture. When Martin was 9 years old, he talked my mother into allowing him to take a bee course at Utah State. The professor initially said "No" because he felt he was too young, but Martin was persistent; the professor finally agreed on the condition that my mom enroll under her name, and Martin could "sit in" on the class with her. When he finished the class, he and dad built their first beehive, and that's how this all got started. In the early '90s Martin decided it was time to make bees his business and he wanted us all to be involved.

"Business, more than any other occupation, is a continual dealing with the future; it is a continual calculation, an instinctive exercise in foresight."
– Henry R. Luce

My dad, Elmer James, is CEO and executive engineer of the Slide Ridge clan, designing and inventing the equipment for our facilities, making it easier to reach our dreams. My mom, Jean, contributes to our Honey Wine Vinegar recipe development, cooks lunch, and feeds everyone who is at the office on any given day, including visitors and vendors. My job is resident artist and graphic designer. I'm responsible for the presentation of our Slide Ridge image and branding. I also manage the office, order fulfillment, coordination of sales, and customer relationships. Karla, my sister, is the ultimate beekeeper extraordinaire; she spends many hours outdoors with the bees, and in her spare time takes care of the books and helps with sales. Our brother, Mike, is chief mechanic and maintenance specialist, keeping all equipment and processes running smoothly. And Martin is the dreamer, company founder, head beekeeper, and creator of our handcrafted Honey Wine Vinegar and Honey Wines. My daughter, Krisa, is warehouse and production assistant; she works the summer farmers' market circuit to help sell and promote our product. Karla's daughter, Taleen, developed and produces our Bee Simple product line that blends beeswax with essential oils to become lotions and lip balm; she also helps with the honey extraction. Jerrica, Martin's daughter, works the warehouse and production as well. And my daughter-in-law, Shaunie, is responsible for all production, assembling orders, and kitchen maintenance. It takes all of us to keep this company going!

## 7 Points on Bee Products:

1. An average hive in Utah produces 32 pounds of honey per year (varies widely based on the season).
2. 1 quart of honey is 3 pounds.
3. It takes 12 bees their whole lives to produce 1 teaspoon of honey.
4. The average life span of a bee during honey flow is 30 days.
5. A queen bee, by weight, is worth more than gold.
6. Bees will consume 8–12 pounds of honey to produce 1 pound of beeswax.
7. It takes 18–24 months to produce a single batch of Honey Wine Vinegar.

Slide Ridge has been a company since 2004. We started out with 200 hives and have built up to about 2,500 hives. When we began we were strictly doing pollination and the honey was just a by-product. During the winter it's hard to keep bees here in Utah because of the cold. We transport the bees ourselves via semi-truck (Martin, Karla, and I all have commercial drivers licenses) to a holding yard in Nevada where they stay for a month or so; then they go to California to pollinate the almond groves; and afterward they head back to Nevada and stay until spring. They come back to Utah for the summer and go to work in the orchards in Cache Valley, gathering nectar, pollen, and building up the hives. By late summer, the bee colonies are large enough to gather the excess honey that is the core of our business. By fall, the hives are full and we can begin extraction of the honey and start creating our products. Pollen is collected from the wild flowers high in the mountains of Utah; it produces an extremely unique, elite-quality raw honey that is pure, unfiltered nectar.

# The most valuable business lesson I can pass along is to make sure you get a good education and to always think positive.

We became a winery because we wanted to make vinegar; we make Honey Wine Vinegar that has a distinctive, sweet, smooth flavor so tasty you can drink it! We even put it in our water bottles in the summer; it is very healthy for you, helps keep you hydrated, keeps your ph. in balance, and, best of all, it's totally natural. And it's not only great for salad dressings, my husband, Dave, also makes an incredible marinade for chicken, pork, and beef that he then tosses on the barbeque. We also have a new vinegar flavor made from our CaCysir Wine that will be called Harvest Apple Vinegar; it is created from locally grown apples mixed with our honey. I'm working on label designs now and the bottles will be shipped to us in a month or so.

We have a lot of plans for the future. Something that's very important to us is to help out other agricultural farmers, which is why we made the apple vinegar; we found that a lot of local orchard crops were just going to waste. Part of being a sustainable business is helping others around us. We are also working on several more flavors for our line of products, but I'm not allowed to say what those are yet — they are top secret!

**END**

# ANDREA BRICCO

Andrea Bricco is a bright, shining star in the world of food photography. Formerly from Wisconsin, she now makes her home in an artist's loft in the heart of downtown Los Angeles. Her work is true and honest, vibrant, and visually descriptive ... more reminiscent of fine art than food portraiture.

When I was growing up we lived in the country, so food was very central to my family. We had a garden, we canned and pickled, and made beef jerky and maple syrup from scratch. There was always a copy of *Bon Appétit* magazine laying around. When I was 17 years old I decided to go to school to be a food photographer, which sort of came out of nowhere. At that point in my life I had never even owned a camera, but the idea seemed to make sense to me. I started college in 2000, enrolled in classes, bought all the required books, and purchased my camera. While my classmates were doing portraiture, I was in the corner taking shots of salads!

I've been photographing food for about 13 years. I attended a two-year program in Madison, Wisconsin, and I had an internship at a photo studio while I was in college. After college I worked freelance at Land's End for a year, which turned into a full-time job for another year, and then I moved to Los Angeles.

"Timing, perseverance, and 10 years of trying will eventually make you look like an overnight success."
— Biz Stone

Wanting more opportunities, specifically in food photography, I knew Los Angeles was the place I needed to be to make that happen. When I moved here I had to start all over again. I took assisting jobs with celebrity, fashion, and food photographers to learn more and gain experience. I did this for about six years, soaking up as much knowledge as possible. I didn't have the luxury of starting out with money, so I had to work during the day and develop my portfolio at night. There eventually came a point when I was receiving enough job offers that I was able to leave assisting behind. It was a nerve-racking thing to do, but I had to trust that it was the right move for me to make.

When I first started out, I was very anxious to have everything right away: a big studio, great jobs, and the best equipment. I soon realized that I needed to relax my expectations, work hard, and keep at it. There is a saying that really makes sense to me now: "You can't become an expert at anything until you've been doing it for at least 10 years."

For the past few years I have shot mainly on location at different restaurants, and when I needed a large studio I'd rent one. Lately I've been getting enough work that I began to need my own studio, so I recently moved into a new studio that is large enough for me to live and work in.

Food has always been my primary focus — all of the other stuff was just to make a living. I've realized that if you're experienced in 10 different areas you may be seen as a jack-of-all-trades, but it can also be confusing for prospective clients. I made the conscious decision to market myself strictly as a food photographer. In this field especially, you are hired based on your unique look and style. It's up to you to create a statement and show clients your vision.

I'm currently in the process of working on a cookbook with Alicia Buszczak, who is an incredible prop and food stylist in L.A. The book will include recipes, but in large part it will focus on how the photos are taken and styled, making it a very different kind of cookbook. I am also working with various editorial clients, including Wolfgang Puck, *Los Angeles* magazine, King's Hawaiian Bakery, Delta's *Sky* magazine, *Where Women Cook,* and *Country Woman* magazine, as well as many restaurants too. I'd eventually like to have a larger studio that is devoted solely to work, and I really need to get an agent at some point — it's not easy doing everything myself!

In the future I hope to work on more cookbooks. Chefs are amazing artists, and each plated dish is like a piece of edible artwork. As a food photographer, my job is to capture perfectly what a chef has created, which is really fun. I think looking at food is such a huge part of enjoying it … almost as much as eating it!

**END**

# ALICIA BUSZCZAK

Alicia Buszczak is an artist and prop stylist living and working in Los Angeles, California. She was born in Connecticut and spent a large part of her youth living in South Africa. Traveling throughout Africa and Europe with her family shaped her unique aesthetic and interest in social activism. Alicia holds a degree in art history and enjoys politics, literature, nature, and painting. She firmly believes that we each make our own luck.

I have been seeking out visual balance for as long as I can remember. When I was a child, my mother collected small objects on her dressing table, a group of hand-carved elephants being my favorite. I would move them around as she put on her makeup, trying new compositions and patterns with the members of the herd. This act of play was probably my first foray into styling.

I became incredibly interested in the relationships between objects and their surroundings and how those juxtapositions made me feel. That theme has continued to be a present and driving force throughout my life.

I took to painting very young and enrolled in every art class that was available. By high school I was making a practice of truly looking at life's compositions and how people arranged themselves and their belongings in various environs: on buses, waiting in lines, or in their offices and homes. In fact, I found I had such an interest in design that I wanted to study it further in college. This led me to study art history in an attempt to further understand how the visual world operates. The long lectures held me captive, and I began to see patterns and make connections between eras and movements in the world around me. Upon graduation I moved to New York City with the hopes of working at a museum or gallery, but something far more tactile was in store for me.

I had been living in the city for a few months when a friend shared an ad she had found in The Times; ABC Carpet & Home was looking for a new visual merchandiser. We had spent long hours together drifting through the antiques and fabrics of that beautiful store on Broadway, and she convinced me to call for an interview. Thankfully, I got the job — and it was heaven. There were painters who created enormous backdrops, designers who crafted the perfect props, and an electrician whose sole task was to make the grand, antique chandeliers that arrived each month from Europe come back to life. A year into my working there, ABC opened two new restaurants and a food market, which included a fishmonger, a cheese shop, and a bakery. A

spark was lit inside me. The food, its packaging, the aromas, and infinite possibilities for transformation captivated me. I had discovered something that spoke to me on the same raw level of the elephants on my mother's dressing table.

I had segued into styling for still photography when a friend who was an art director for a large menswear retailer needed an extra stylist for a catalogue shoot. I was happy to try, and I found that new world to be as fascinating as my art history lectures and visual merchandising combined. One shoot led to another, and I began to focus on making a life for myself working on still sets; however, I continued to search for my perfect fit within that world.

"In order to be irreplaceable, one must always be different."
– Coco Chanel

I found my place working with food and props on commercial and editorial food shoots. In one place, at one time, are all the tools and opportunities I needed to create something truly special.

Food is as essential to life as breath, water, and perhaps even love. When I think of the people I have so often watched while looking for inspiration, I realize that they almost always had food; it is a common ground, filled with emotion and vitality. Within the still food photography set there are infinite possibilities for a stylist to explore, from the surfaces to the dishes and glassware — everything that touches the food tells its story.

I have learned to trust my instincts above all else. If something doesn't feel right, there's a reason — this holds as true on set as it does off. The only way to hone this skill is to watch, to listen, to constantly observe, and practice what you love; for me, this is design, people, and food. I am hopelessly in love with what I do for a living. For the future, my plans are ever-expanding. I am currently working on both a cookbook and a new venture called The Surface Library, which will provide rental surfaces and tabletop props for shoots in the greater Los Angeles area.

END

# SUSAN CURTIS

At a time of life when many women slow down to taste the pleasures of retirement, Susan Curtis still simmers with possibilities. As the founder of the Santa Fe School of Cooking, Susan just turned the burners up by moving the business into a sparkling new facility, breathing life into a venerable building in downtown Santa Fe, New Mexico, and expanding the school's ability to do what it does best — sharing the unique regional cuisine of New Mexico with food lovers.

Starting a cooking school was not actually a life-long dream for me, but everything in my life prepared me to succeed. I was raised in the idyllic setting of an Idaho ranch near the banks of the Snake River. Ranch life was a feast of foraging, canning, and baking, and enjoying the cattle, sheep, pigs, chickens, and horses that were a constant in my life. Aided by the incredible cooking skills of my mother and grandmother, what came to our table came from the abundance of the land. Our midday meal was a delicious cornucopia shared with family and the many friends who were always welcome to share the convivial atmosphere. Being thoroughly immersed in the cycle of ranch life gave me an abiding appreciation for the land, the livestock, and the food that resulted from each.

"To laugh often and much; to win the respect of intelligent people and affection of children; to earn the appreciation of honest critics and endure the betrayal of false friends; to appreciate beauty, to find the best in others; to leave the world a bit better, whether by a healthy child, a garden patch, or a redeemed social condition; to know even one life has breathed easier because you have lived. This is to have succeeded."
– Ralph Waldo Emerson

My father planted the seeds of creating a life of one's own; an entrepreneur himself, he created businesses from scratch. From him, I learned that when you start a business, there are no half measures. As a tomboy on the ranch, I assumed I would marry a cowboy and live on the land, but I fell for a musical scientist with a rewarding combination of intellect and good humor. I wanted two things from marriage: to have fun and grow old together. I've been blessed with both, along with two hard-working daughters and four wonderful grandchildren, all living here in Santa Fe.

In 1989, with one daughter in college and another almost there, a classic mid-life crisis hit. My husband, David, and I had taken a trip to New Orleans, where I attended classes at Joe Cahn's New Orleans School of Cooking, igniting a desire to connect my past to the present through food. One cold February night, I shook David awake and told him I wanted to start a cooking school. Within 10 days we were on our way back to New Orleans to consult with Joe, and by December the Santa Fe School of Cooking and Market had opened its doors to share the flavors of New Mexico's unique cuisine, rooted in chile and "The Three Sisters": corn, beans, and squash.

To create a successful business, you must begin with what you enjoy. I was inspired by the specificity of regional cooking everywhere that David and I traveled, and I always brought back cookbooks and serving dishes from around the world. Basically, I just wanted to offer to others what I loved to do.

BUSINESS TIP

Starting a business demands that you have your personal life in order because you have to give it all you've got. It takes blood, sweat, and tears, but I'm grateful that by sharing my love for local food with those who love to cook, the Santa Fe School of Cooking and Market has become an integral part of New Mexico's food traditions.

Santa Fe School of Cooking
Flavors of the Southwest

Susan Curtis and Nicole Curtis Ammerman

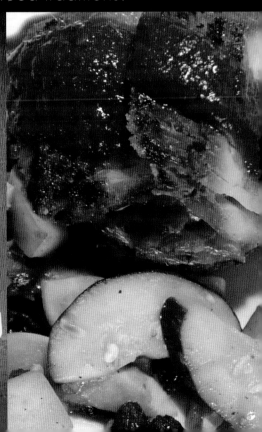

Thorough research is critical; start by visiting existing businesses to provide a roadmap for what you want to do. Since my interest was in regional cooking, I educated myself by meeting with every supplier and local restaurateur I could, going through their warehouses and kitchens and picking their brains. I rented a kitchen and hired a chef to recipe-test in order to develop three representative regional menus. It took three months to develop a solid template, but those menus are still our most popular classes!

In the beginning chefs auditioned for us, and I was open to anyone: home cooks, locals, and moonlighting restaurant chefs. Teaching credentials are nice, and restaurant experience is good, but I look for charismatic personalities who are able to bring the cuisine to life. We have a pool of chefs, coming from both local referrals and those who approach us directly, and it's a win-win for them too; they get the benefit of our marketing, are able to sell their cookbooks, and often pick up catering opportunities as a result of the classes they teach.

Class size generally runs from 12–20 students, but in our new space we can accommodate up to 60 people! A standard single subject, such as salsas, runs 1½ hours, while demonstration and hands-on classes both last about 3 hours. Class volume is heaviest from April through Christmas, and we offer lower-cost bonus classes in the off-season. Traditional New Mexican foods are still the heart and soul of the business, but our roster has expanded. In 2006, we created our popular restaurant walking tours, partnering with many talented local chefs. In 2010, we added a three-day Boot Camp, offering a deeper immersion in southwestern flavors and techniques. For a number of years we were in a break-even position, but we are trying to work smarter now, with a formal analysis based on the total cost of classes in each category and the volume of sales in the market. An intelligent staffing ratio is also imperative.

On the retail side, it's essential to find a niche, and from the start the market was designed to offer a unique line of products not available elsewhere; in fact, some of what we sell arose simply from finding products we needed for the classes. Now we feature everything from stovetop grills for chile roasting to alligator wood cutting boards to black La Chamba cookware that goes straight from oven to table.

The practice of always saying "Yes, yes, we can" let us take a leap of faith in 2012, when we acquired a historic Santa Fe building that was built in the 1940s as a Packard dealership. The expansion gave us a facility specifically designed for a greater number and variety of classes and allowed the market to feature a broader palette of culinary products.

Our growth has been organic. We have enjoyed the support of the food-loving community, with both locals and visitors becoming not just students but also friends. Starting a business means you have to give it all you've got, but I'm grateful that by sharing my love for local food with those who love to cook, the Santa Fe School of Cooking and Market has become an integral part of New Mexico's food traditions.

END

# LISA DUPAR

For nearly 30 years, Seattle-based chef Lisa Dupar has earned a reputation for creating food inspired by her Southern roots while honoring classic techniques and amazing local ingredients. As a child, Lisa ran wild every summer with her cousins in Charleston, South Carolina, where many of her early culinary impressions were formed. Lisa always knew she wanted to be a chef and went directly from high school to a culinary apprenticeship at the Westin Peachtree Plaza in Atlanta. Since then, she has launched two popular restaurants, a successful catering company, and published an IACP award-winning cookbook.

I was raised in a "foodie" Southern family before we knew there was a name for it. As a kid in Charleston, South Carolina, my cousins and I would crab almost daily. I was in good company — all of us kids loved to cook. Our dining room table was crowded with each of us devouring salted cantaloupe, sweet onions, summer tomatoes, or shrimp piled on newspapers alongside bowls of cocktail sauce. My Southern grandmother, Jimmy Todd, always had her kitchen full of benne seed wafers, black walnut cake, pecan tassies, and sweet creek shrimp in piles waiting to be peeled by our helping hands.

My first high school sweetheart had parents right off the boat from Italy. His mother, Mary, was a homemaker who baked and decorated elaborate cakes and made her own sausage and pasta from scratch — this was unheard of in America in the '70s. Completely entranced, I was more interested in visiting her after school than my boyfriend. She spent hours teaching me how to properly pipe icing, roll pastillage, and decorate cakes. While most other high school kids were babysitting, I started decorating cakes to earn spending money.

LISA DUPAR

# fried chicken & champagne

A ROMP THROUGH THE KITCHEN AT POMEGRANATE BISTRO

photos by KATHRYN BARNARD

"I find that the harder I work, the more luck I seem to have."
– Thomas Jefferson

After a three-year culinary apprenticeship at the Peachtree Plaza Hotel in Atlanta, I spent two years cooking in Switzerland. Back in the states, I was transferred to Seattle to help open The Palm Court, a fine dining room in the Westin Hotel. I was the first female chef for the chain at the time. In 1984, I opened my first small restaurant, Southern Accents. Although the restaurant was consistently busy, the price point was too low to draw a salary. I started catering to increase revenues at a time when breaking even felt like a good month. My husband had just been laid off from the only income that was supporting us at the time, and I was five months pregnant with my first child. I thought, "Well, we could always cater to bring in extra income."

By the time I was pregnant with my second child, something had to go. I was cooking on the line each night in the restaurant, taking catering jobs as they came, and deep-cleaning the kitchen on the only day we were closed. Three years into catering, it began to subsidize the restaurant and we realized it had the potential to be a stand-alone business. I closed the restaurant and focused solely on catering.

Steadily over time, we grew the business. We experienced increases in revenue of approximately 10 percent annually for about 10 years; however, six years into catering exclusively, I went through a divorce, became a single mom, and found that my "paycheck" (profits from the business) put my income below the national poverty line at the time. This wake-up call made me realize how little I knew about running my company as a real business. I had my head buried in the cookie dough up until that point. I searched for the most knowledgeable group of advisors I could find. One consultant/life coach I still have today; he pushed me to formulate goals (both personal and business), write a business plan, and taught me how to read a balance sheet. In the course of one year, I doubled my salary.

Little did I know that my first catering job, inspired by the need to pay bills, would lead to the company we have today, more than 28 years later. I hired my current husband, Jonathan Zimmer, as the chef when I realized that running back and forth from the kitchen to the office was counterproductive. With Jonathan's drive and determination, we have grown the company to approximately 300 employees between a new restaurant and catering. Our team is amazing and every day I work with a huge family of friends and colleagues whom I respect tremendously.

END

## Recipe for Success

### Ingredients:

1 part Strong Passion, steeped until robust enough to hold its strength even when more hot water is added!

1 part Crystal Clear Plan

4 Essential Essences

Know your Numbers

Leadership Skills

Stick to Core Competencies

Nurture all Relationships

### Method:

Review and revisit your ingredient list monthly. Do better each year. Be open to the possibility that there is always a better recipe. Be a student of all new ingredients for improvement.

# KRISTEN FIELDS

Austin, Texas, is an up-and-coming epicenter for foodies and hipsters. It is a vibrant city very much alive with a food culture all its own. Entrepreneurs Kristen and Cody Fields own and operate mmmpanadas. They are gourmet, artisan empanada makers using only fresh ingredients to create tantalizing, unexpected flavor combinations, savory or sweet, whatever your taste. Voted one of the 10 Best Food Trucks in America by *GQ* Magazine, mmmpanadas is quickly gaining street cred!

Before I met my husband, Cody, I was teaching a Pilates class in a studio in West Austin, where I've lived off and on for the past 20 years. With a background in modern dance I really never expected to find myself making and selling empanadas for a living, but here I am and I'm really loving it! I met Cody when he was in Austin visiting friends; he had just quit his job in Costa Rica and was taking a year off. He decided to move back to Austin so we could be together, but he had to take a job that he didn't like at all. During this time he was always talking about these empanadas that he used to eat every day in Costa Rica. The first time he mentioned empanadas, I didn't even know what they were.

After he made some for me, I was like, "Yeah, yeah those are pretty good!" Two years went by and all the while Cody was hating his job and talking nonstop about empanadas. We hadn't really considered the possibility of actually doing something with them.

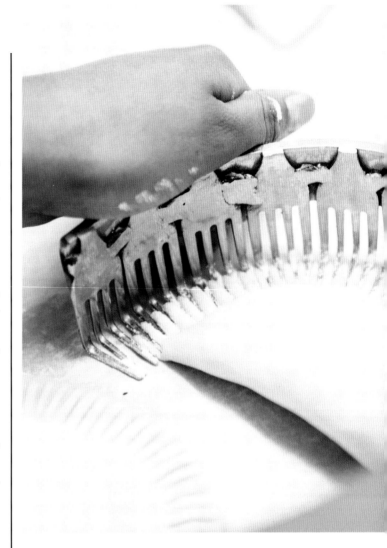

"Eighty percent of success is showing up."
– Woody Allen

One night we were at a neighborhood bar talking to the owner. Out of the blue, I asked him if they had empanadas on the menu. He said, "Oh, my empanada guy fell through," and I said that he had to try our mmmpanadas, that they are the most amazing ones he'd ever eat. At this point, I had yet to make one myself — I was just testing the waters, opening my mouth to see what would happen and what would come back at me. To my total surprise the guy said, "I'd like to try those!" The next day I went shopping for all the ingredients we needed to make up a batch. Cody and I made them together and took them over to the bar, feeling half silly about just showing up with food. The owner was very receptive and promptly placed an order. We went

out and got our licensing and filed the necessary paperwork to get our LLC, mmmpanadas, started right then and there.

We rented a shared commercial kitchen for an hourly rate and started making empanadas one night a week. For the first three years, I was teaching my Pilates class from 7 a.m. to 2 p.m. and then I'd go to the kitchen at 4 p.m. to work until midnight. Our empanadas are handmade, with Cody and I pressing them together one fork tine mark at a time. I had to make a real commitment, taking the risk to leave my day job and really do this. I knew I needed to be able to put more into it so we could get more out of it. It was the right decision.

In 2008 we bought a food truck. I thought it would be a good marketing tool, a way to establish our brand. I wanted to stake our claim as an entity in a very obvious way. Now there is a big food truck movement and it's really been great for our business.

Our packaged empanadas are now sold in select Whole Foods; however, these don't have our branding on them. Since we are self-funded, an easy growth step was to use very simple packaging, so we ship them frozen in cardboard boxes to stores where they sell them hot in their grab-and-go delis. We are currently designing the packaging for our retail line. Our goal is to be in the frozen food section with our own product, and we are looking at expanding.

Over the past five years we have built our business and our brand — we love what we do and take a lot of pride in it. It is really important for us to have a quality product that doesn't look like it was spit out of a machine!

**END**

mmmpanadas

austin, tx | gourmet empanadas

www.mmmpanadas.com

Did y'all know that
thinks we're great!

BUSINESS TIP

Had I known earlier in life that this is what I'd be doing, I would have enrolled in business courses immediately. We are fortunate that Austin has one of the best small business entrepreneurship programs in the country, which offers classes at a very low cost. It has been a super resource and I've taken several courses over the years.

# ABBY FREETHY

Chef Abby Freethy lives in the scenic Moosehead Lake region of Maine. Her company, Northwoods Gourmet Girl, produces an elegant line of all-natural, healthy pantry staples, one delectable jar at a time. Abby's goal is to raise awareness about the importance of adopting a healthy lifestyle, beginning with proper nutrition, but that doesn't have to mean bland — far from it! She creates delicious Wild Maine Blueberry Jam, heavenly Cherry Tartlet Preserves, spicy Jalapeno Ketchup, zesty Habanero Relish, Caramelized Balsamic Onions, and, the one that started it all, mouth-watering Country Ketchup.

I am originally from Pennsylvania and have a very large, loud, and hysterical extended family. Our lives have always revolved around the kitchen — we like to have fun and eat. I cook the same way all my grandmothers did: from scratch, with a few added twists of my own. It's important to me to keep things pure. I live in a place that's very rural. It's so beautiful here — situated on one of the largest, most pristine lakes — it's the epitome of what you'd think the North Woods should be. In this area you really have to create your own job, which makes you take risks or you just become part of the status quo, and that's never been me.

I've been a chef for 23 years and have always been interested in all-natural, organic food, even before it was all the rage. When I was pregnant with my son, Dustin, in 2005, the only thing I could keep down was French fries and ketchup. I knew there were preservatives and added sugars in the ketchup I was eating and thought I could make my own healthier version.

*Gour...*

MaineWomen Working Together

www.clov.com

I was working in a restaurant at the time, and I decided to start up a little cottage industry. I had my home kitchen certified so that I could produce certain pantry goods, and I began experimenting with different formulations of my ketchup recipe. I had my son in September, and the following year I got really serious, put a plan together, and went into a commercial space. The Northwoods Gourmet Girl brand was born.

We started with ketchup and quickly moved on to more products. I wanted to create something a bit more sophisticated, like charred onion ketchup and jalapeno ketchup, and soon more pantry staples came along like relishes, jams, and dessert sauces. My belief is that you should always be able to taste the first ingredient. At this point we had 25 products and opened a little café in the front of the building. Our menu reflected our condiments, like a buffalo meatloaf sandwich with charred onion mashed potatoes drenched in a sauce made from my ketchup. The restaurant became very popular, but we started to lose sight of what we were originally doing. I wanted to make products, not run a café. I made the decision to back up a little bit, and then just kept plugging away.

We remained in that building until last year, and we have now built a new production facility; it is a beautiful, functional, unencumbered space. There is a giant tower in the middle of the building and its top floor is specifically for my son. I wanted to create a safe place for him to play while I am downstairs working.

It seems that we are becoming a line of products now, not just foods. I have a background in art and design, and I've always worn my own unique take on a chef's uniform, consisting of the traditional jacket, a little skirt, which is especially comfortable in a hot kitchen, leggings, pants, and a wrap dress. I had the idea to create really cute chefs' clothing, so I designed a group of adorable A-line skirts and matching jackets. It is all very exciting!

---

## 4 Points on Expanding Your Product Line:

1. If you decide to expand your product line you need to be certain to keep the main focus of your business on your existing brand. This means the new line must be promoted/sold through your established channels. If the new line is outside of your current manufacturing capabilities, be careful to completely understand the new manufacturing industry that you are entering. As an example: Because of my previous education, we are adding a new clothing line that we will sell initially only in our own retail store. The production is different, easier than food, but the sales are to the same retailer and consumer.

2. Create a new promotional piece, such as a catalog, to highlight your new product line, but continue to promote your existing line. This catalog can be viewed online or printed and distributed to current customers.

3. Pursue additional means of promoting both your new product and existing product. For example: TV, expanded social media, magazine features.

4. Plan a "debut" of the new product as a means of highlighting the new line as well as promoting your existing line. Such debuts can take place at trade shows, online, and in local or national restaurants or retail stores.

Northwoods Gourmet Girl products are in countless stores throughout Maine and we are in negotiations with Crate and Barrel. We are even producing wood kiosks and interesting little tables to display our goods. I'm very tied to my community, and I am proud to say that I've created five jobs in this tiny town.

I've always had this enormous vision of what I wanted my company to be, and reaching that goal has been a step-by-step process. I know how difficult it can be to make everything work, especially if you're not always sure where the next paycheck is going to come from. It feels like a huge accomplishment to be here ... where what I have dreamed about is starting to come true!

END

**Northwoods Gourmet Girl,** *Northwoods Gourmet Girl,* Northw

Northwoods Gourmet Girl 14oz
# Maine Cranberry Relish
*All natural & not too sweet*
2 Depot Street, Greenville Junction, Maine. 04441
Northwoodsgourmetgirl.com/207.570.8112
Maine cranberries, Fresh OJ, orange zest, cane sugar, pectin
*Proudly made in the Northwoods of Maine*

Northwoods Gourmet Girl 1=
SWEET&SPICY TOASTED WALNUTS
MAINE SEA SALT
*Maine made products working together*
203 Pritham Avenue , Greenville Maine. 04441
Northwoodsgourmetgirl.com/207.570.8112
Walnuts, cane sugar, egg white, sea salt, h2o, cayenne pepper

# CONNIE GREEN

If you love all things natural and enjoy being in the great outdoors, then you too can live vicariously through famed wild mushroom hunter Connie Green. Situated in the extraordinarily beautiful setting of Napa, California, she set the stage for a great renaissance in American cooking in the late '70s — a movement that began in the San Francisco Bay Area and quickly spread across the country. Connie pioneered the popularity of wild foods by providing some of the best chefs in the United States with one of their most precious and beloved ingredients.

"Wrinkles should merely indicate where smiles have been."
– Mark Twain

## How to Create an Entire Industry from Your Passion:

1. Beginning as a solo forager blessed with wonderously rich chanterelle patches, there began the process of finding others in the West with the same passion and pride in picking beautiful mushroooms. Now, unlike most mushroom companies, we actually pick the mushrooms ourselves. A network of great mushroom pickers has been woven across the West, Canada, Alaska, Mexico, and even Europe.

2. We are dedicated to something rarely achieved in the wild mushroom world. The unparalleled quality of our mushrooms begins in the forest with the discriminating and proud eyes of skilled pickers. Picking cleanly and selectively is where all quality begins.

3. In this wacky business where stone-age hunter-gatherer tradition crosses paths with haute cuisine, sustainability is the secret ingredient. As evidence mounts that mushroom picking actually increases mushroom fruiting, people are finally coming to understand that gathering mushrooms is analogous to harvesting fruit from long-lived trees.

4. Long ago I wrote in an article that commercial mushroom hunting can give a living back to loggers and make our forests economically more valuble in the long term if left standing than if converted to lumber. Numerous small Pacific Northwest towns have worked to stop the clear-cutting of forest tracts that provide locals with additional income from mushroom gathering. It is our goal to match our zealousness in providing chefs with mushrooms of exceptional beauty with the same zealousness in preserving the wild country from which they come.

I've never been able to do things the easy way — I think that's a pretty standard way of life for most entrepreneurs. I feel I'm more animal than the average human, mainly because my ability to sit still and stay indoors is extremely limited. It's a natural state for me to be wandering, browsing, and looking at the world, and what I do for a living is simply a consequence of that. As a little kid, I felt very lucky to live in a swampy area of Florida where an ice-age lake had once existed; I would find all kinds of bones from Mastodons and Glyptodons. My mother also grew up in wild country, so she didn't worry about me when I was out roaming around. She raised me to believe that nature was a familiar friend.

In the late '70s, I met and married my late husband, Tony, who was from Eastern Europe. As a little boy during WWII, he had to forage for food to survive and avoid starvation. He introduced me to the world of wild mushrooms and after that it was all over! Finding food for the table was my calling. It seemed my whole life had been designed for this purpose, no question about it, and best of all I was extremely good at it. I had this innate ability to find great quantities of mushrooms, and I soon realized they had the potential to be a highly prized commodity to many a chef.

By 1980 I began introducing them to local chefs, but at that time most American kitchens weren't accustomed to wild foods yet, so it wasn't easy. I figured European chefs would be the best place to start. The first chef I met with was a Frenchman; he looked at me and said, "Chanterelles don't grow in this country!" Slowly but surely I made my way through Napa and San Francisco Bay Area kitchens. I was in the right place at the right time, just at the beginning of a renaissance in American cuisine. The old guard of fancy French restaurants was giving way to an explosion of a new breed of young, "California Fresh" style chefs — and it really all started right here in San Francisco.

I began to expand my hunting territory. After Chanterelle season, I moved on to Morels in the spring and then to Porcinis up in the mountains and on the coast. It was natural to start working with other mushroom pickers to be able to supply more restaurants, and inexplicably it turned into a business: Wine Forest Wild Foods.

I feel very fortunate to have been a part of that movement. It was a very exciting time and still is, and my career has been on an incredible trajectory ever since. I've been at this business for about 33 years, and I've had the privilege of working with some of the greatest chefs in the United States. My book, "The Wild Table" (Studio, 2010), came about through my association with Chef Thomas Keller — his belief in me has been profoundly helpful. It has been an extraordinary labor of love and I couldn't be happier with it.

My passion and absolute joy is providing an array of wild and "tamed" food products to American households, which are available on my website. My goal is to raise my customers' expectations by educating them about the unpredictable nature of wild foods so they can better understand the mystique and romance of a wild harvest and how we must work in harmony with nature in order to obtain this. I want people to know that you don't have to be a great chef to make great food!

END

the
wild table

seasonal foraged food
and recipes

Connie
Green
and
SARAH SCOTT
foreword by
Thomas Keller

# SUSIE HOLT

For many years, boutique owner Susie Holt would spend time in her kitchen as a means to escape her hectic life in retail. Today that escape is now a part of her hectic life ... and she wouldn't have it any other way. After 15 successful years, Susie's charming home décor shop, Posh on Palm, now includes a delightful café and bakery. Cooking and baking aren't her only means of escape; after all, she and her husband, Mark, live in an amazing 1920s cottage on the shores of the Gulf of Mexico, on a tiny little island paradise called Casey Key — a truly glorious place to get away from the hustle and bustle of the real world.

Posh on Palm is our home away from home. It has been a long and winding road that led us to where we are today. It all began 16 years ago with a dream and an ice cream cone. Mark, my wonderful husband, came home from a long and stressful day of work. He was a very talented goldsmith and it was the heart of the Christmas shopping season ... need I say more? I had been working long days as a designer, and I was all too aware that we both needed a breather. We headed to downtown Venice to relax over an ice cream cone, and as we strolled down the street toward the parlor I saw that the shop in one of my favorite storefronts was going out of business. We took a peek inside and then continued toward our destination. It was a beautiful evening, so we sat on a bench enjoying the quiet and our cold treats. I began to daydream out loud about how much I would love to quit my job and open my own boutique in that storefront shop.

As we talked I began to get more and more excited, sharing with Mark all of my ideas. He perked up a little at the thought of leaving his stressful work environment. The conversation continued and our energy totally changed. We were so involved in creating this vision that we didn't notice the man who sat down an earshot away and was clearly caught up in our conversation too. As fate would have it, he owned the building! Out of curiosity, we inquired about the space. As one of the best locations within the heart of the antiques district, there was a waiting list for the building. I was crushed, but we continued on sharing our ideas. The man hesitated for a moment and then said, "Give me $50 as a deposit and the space is yours." And so it began, the beginning of our wonderful adventure.

FAVORITE QUOTE

"Love of beauty is taste. The creation of beauty is art."
— Ralph Waldo Emerson

We were afraid to leave the security of our careers, but we were more excited about creating this world that we share today. Mark is an excellent woodworker and craftsman, and I design our exquisite linens. Together we have a passion for creating beautiful spaces within our shop and for our clients and friends. We had a long and wonderful run in Venice until the building sold, which brought us to the amazing location where we are today. It is a historic hotel in downtown Sarasota complete with the original pressed-tin ceilings and marble floors. We set up shop and fell in love with our new home.

Life was cruising on autopilot when we began waffling over a very difficult decision. Our formula had always worked for us, and we were fortunate to have a very loyal following, but we felt like we could still do more. Changes in the economy were making noticeable fluctuations in the world of retail, and we felt like we could make a positive adjustment to our plan. I have always had a passion for baking,

but never really felt like I could possibly work more hours in a day. After much discussion, we decided to add an old-fashioned bakery counter and small café into our boutique shop. Mark immediately jumped into action and began creating walls and building a kitchen. It was a gamble, but we have never strayed from a challenge.

I wanted the lines between the retail shop and the café to be seamless, so we decorated the dining area just like the shop. All the tables and chairs are mix-and-match vintage pieces with beautiful linens, and there are ironstone pitchers for flowers on every table. Our serving dishes are vintage floral plates, cups, and saucers in every charming style we could find. We have also expanded outward, offering delightful alfresco dining. The concept for the menu was not a stretch for me. I bake the childhood favorites that my mother and grandmother taught me how to make when I was knee-high, and those recipes for carrot cake and coconut cake are our hottest sellers today.

If you ask me if I would change anything, the answer would be "No." We work twice as hard and are twice as exhausted, but we are also happier than ever. The café has brought so many more people through our door, and we are surrounded by a lot of smiling faces. It is a joy and a blessing to be so fortunate. We may work harder than ever before, but it makes us appreciate our little beachfront paradise that much more as well. I am, and always will be, a beach girl. The sights and the sounds not only bring me peace but also inspire me to get up the next day and create something else of beauty. Our inspiring surroundings are so evident in everything we do.

As our world continues to change around us, we try to find ways to adapt. Our next adventure for Posh on Palm is to expand upward! I mentioned that Posh is located in an old hotel … well, it is our dream to now renovate the upper floor and offer 14 beautiful rooms in our future boutique-style bed and breakfast. We dream big and are always encouraging one another. I work with the love of my life, we share our passion for creating beautiful things, and we can sit with our toes in the sand and watch the sunset before we say goodnight. Our life has been a wonderful journey, and I wouldn't change a thing.

END

Moving our business to Sarasota was very easy for us. We have been an established business for years, so we already had a huge clientele that follows us wherever we go. Many of our customers live in Sarasota, so it actually became easier for them to come to us. We have settled very well into this new community, and we have found a younger clientele. The cafe' has been all word of mouth so far, and we are doing great. There are a lot of condos and businesses nearby that really support us. We feel so blessed to have found such an amazing location as well as an amazing building. We appreciate every single customer we have and never take them for granted. We love what we do ... it truly is our passion.

# CHERYL ALTERS JAMISON

Globe-trotting authors and outdoor cooking experts Cheryl and Bill Jamison reside in sunny Santa Fe, New Mexico. This adventurous culinary team has collaborated on 16 cookbooks, and counting, many of which have been awarded top honors from the prestigious James Beard Foundation and the International Association of Culinary Professionals. Cheryl is the contributing culinary editor for *New Mexico* magazine and writes a flavorful blog called Tasting New Mexico.

I am interested in a wide range of things and I'm always learning. Food has been a lifelong preoccupation and I pursue culinary knowledge with a real passion, so far as to have developed an entire career around it. I write about food culturally, in terms of recipes and cookbooks, and I also instruct classes.

I'm a Midwest girl, having grown up in Illinois. As a child I was fortunate that my grandmothers were wonderful cooks; they took great interest in teaching me and let me spend time in the kitchen alongside them. My parents always had a garden and they taught me the importance of having good, quality, fresh food that was readily available. I enjoyed discovering all I could about a variety of foods, but I never saw it as something I could do professionally; the only food professional I was aware of was a home economics teacher.

"You'll never know everything about anything, especially something you love."
– Julia Child

When I went to college in Salzburg, Austria, for my junior year, I realized that I particularly enjoyed cuisine as a part of traveling. Traveling around Europe, seeing such a range in the way people cooked and especially the way food was savored, prompted me to think about it in a broader way. Yet I still didn't quite make the career connection.

I went on to receive a master's degree in arts management. I was involved in arts administration, fundraising for nonprofit organizations and developing programs for the next 20 years. During this time my relaxation was to come home and chop vegetables, knead bread, and cook something. I always kept that fascination with food, but it was strictly avocational. It was my husband, Bill, who set me on my current path. Bill was travel-writing at the time and he enlisted my help. Inevitably, our books include a great deal about food because we agree that it is one of the best experiences of traveling the

world. Food is a prime way to get a real look into another culture, not to mention that when the subject of food arises virtually everyone opens up!

It was through this process of travel writing that we decided to do a one-time food book just for fun. I left my job in 1990 to do this full time, as we had been receiving some recognition for the travel books we had written. Since we lived in New Mexico, we thought it fitting to do something that related to New Mexican culture, which has a very distinctive style of cooking. In the Chimayo Valley in northern New Mexico, there is a fabulous restaurant run by an original settling family whose ancestors have been here for over three centuries — *The Rancho de Chimayo Cookbook* (Harvard Common Press, 1991) was the result. The book got a tremendous amount of attention and made us think that maybe we should write one more cookbook, just to get it out of our systems.

## 7 Steps on How to Create a Cookbook:

1. Have a subject that you are both knowledgeable and passionate about — not just interested in, passionate about! That has to come through in the writing.

2. Develop your own voice. There may be a bazillion books out on the same topic as yours, so yours has to stand out and truly come across as special.

3. Think about what publisher and audience would be interested in your book, and why. Know the competition.

4. You will need to seek out an agent if you want to take a book proposal to a "major" publishing house. An agent takes a percentage cut of a book's income, but a good agent will help you get more money (often through creative ways) than you can negotiate on your own. If you consider the self-publishing route, think about how the book will get known and distributed.

5. Put together a cohesive grouping of recipes with a theme.

6. Be relentless about testing recipes. Then test them again.

7. Be prepared to promote the book yourself through social media, cooking classes, special culinary events, and anything else relevant to the topic. The days of publishers doing extensive and extended publicity are gone. You are your own best advocate.

Our next cookbook was *Texas Home Cooking* (Harvard Common Press, 1992), a collection of BBQ, Tex Mex, and traditional Southern-style recipes. We found that we really loved the process of being in the kitchen, doing the research, and working with the food; it quickly became our primary interest. Then came *The Border Cookbook* (Harvard Common Press, 1995), which was the winner of a James Beard Award for Excellence and a finalist for a Julia Child Award in 1996. Many more followed, including *Smoke & Spice* (Harvard Common Press, 2003), which is still in print and to date has sold almost 1 million copies; it was also nominated and won a James Beard Award. We knew that we were really on to something, and it just became our business.

We just turned in our 16th cookbook, and we have a few more books in the works. The Rancho de Chimayo restaurant will be celebrating its 50th anniversary in 2015, and is still run by the same woman; although she is now 80, she is full of energy and wants to do an anniversary edition of the original cookbook to kick off their celebrations. I've had the great fortune of accomplishing many of the things I wanted to do career wise, and I have loved learning something new with each book. In the last nine years we've put out nine books, so we are now ready to slow things down a bit. After all, I think learning is a lifelong process and I want to be able to continue soaking it all in and enjoying everything life has to offer.

**END**

# SHARELLE KLAUS

Sharelle Klaus is an energetic and driven woman who loves her family and her company, Seattle-based DRY Soda Co. Sharelle has reimagined what soda can be: less sweet, fewer calories, with distinctive fruit, flower, and herbal flavors that set her innovative product apart. As a mother of four children, she is continuously on the go, but in her rare spare time she also enjoys running, body surfing, reading, eating fine food, and cooking with her kids.

I launched DRY Soda in 2005 with a thirst for interesting non-alcoholic beverages and a drive to start a revolution within the soda category. From my home office, I set out to redefine an industry, one unique flavor at a time. I'm a food and wine aficionado, and while pregnant with my fourth child I realized that the options for an exciting non-alcoholic beverage were limited — that was my impetus for creating DRY. In the beginning, I sold DRY's first four flavors to Seattle's top restaurants, and soon realized that there was a much larger, and growing, demand for better-tasting and better-for-you sodas. Within the first six months of launch, I began selling DRY to Seattle-area retailers.

"The value of a man resides in what he gives
and not in what he is capable of receiving."
– Albert Einstein

I am the founder of DRY Soda and serve as its CEO. I'm involved in all aspects of the company, from creative to the tactical, and have a great team; we all work together to help bring DRY Soda to as many people as possible. I am a supporter of entrepreneurship and am often a guest speaker at the University of Washington's Foster School of Business, and I judge for the business plan competitions. I'm also on the Executive Committee of the Seattle Pacific University Business School, and I am a member of the Board of Directors of the Seattle Chamber of Commerce.

Over the past few years, DRY Soda has experienced significant growth, which allows us to continue to expand our distribution throughout the country. It is exciting to see the demand for DRY throughout the U.S. and the excitement about a healthier soda.

## Hire people with integrity and generous souls, then you will have an unstoppable team!

Consumers are becoming more educated and conscious of wholesome products and we are meeting that demand through expanded distribution in natural and traditional grocery retailers as well as restaurants, cafés, and bars. DRY Soda is a soda for everyone, and we're working hard to make DRY available everywhere so our customers can have a better soda to choose.

DRY is a refreshing non-alcoholic beverage and also makes a great cocktail mixer. Some of the top mixologists and craft distilleries in Las Vegas, Southern California, and the Pacific Northwest are using DRY in their cocktails and we're thrilled to be part of these innovative cocktail programs. We are really excited about our recent announcement that Chef Richard Blais, Bravo's "Top Chef: All Stars" winner, restaurateur, and author, has been named creative director of DRY Soda. In this role he will work with the company on flavor, recipe, and cocktail innovation as well as serving as a culinary ambassador for the natural soda brand. I love his innovative use of flavors and how he's making exciting food healthful and accessible to the home cook.

I've learned a lot since I started this whole endeavor; for instance, to get out of my own way. When you are new to an industry, it can become challenging to believe in your own instincts and not give too much credit to "industry leaders." Always listen and learn, but never discount your own knowledge, experience, and instincts.

**END**

## 8 Questions to Consider Before Starting a Company

1. Can I get this company funded?
2. Will it be a $100 million company? If not, am I OK with that? Can I fund this company myself (it's difficult to get investors for companies that don't have the $100 million trajectory)?
3. Are there consumer and industry trends that support my idea?
4. Are there any roadblocks in getting my idea to consumers (i.e. distribution, manufacturing, raw materials)?
5. What kind of company culture do I want to create?
6. What do I want the end game of this company to be?
7. What does the balance sheet look like over the first five years?
8. Do I have what it takes to face all the challenges that starting a company entails?

# CHRISTEN KUGENER

Busy wife and mother of two, Christen Kugener, along with her husband, Vincent, own and operate the confections factory Le Caramel, located in Santee, California. They use a traditional French recipe handed down from one of the best caramel makers in France. Time and care is taken to specially handcraft each small batch, which reveals a richly unique flavor and creamy texture. Using simple ingredients like crème fraiche, sugar, sea salt, and butter, they create the most deliciously delightful caramel morsels you have ever tasted.

"When life gives you lemons, make lemonade!"
– Elbert Hubbarb

I am half French and half American, and from a very early age I have always had a sweet tooth, like almost every woman I know. I went to business school in France and immediately after graduating I began a career in finance. While my job was satisfying, it wasn't exactly what I wanted to do for the rest of my life — I had always seen myself as an entrepreneur of sorts with a passion for sweets.

I believe it was serendipity that set me on the path I'm traveling now. My father is a doctor in France, and one day a new patient came in for a checkup; he was Monsieur Palix, the founder of Normandie Caramel, which is the best-selling caramel company in France. He had just retired and mentioned to my dad that he was looking for someone to share his knowledge with … young people who would be interested in learning his techniques and willing to take over all of his recipes so that such a great tradition wouldn't be lost. At this time I was still in college; although I was intrigued and very interested, I wasn't able to make a solid commitment yet.

I met my husband, Vincent, soon after graduation. We were both working in finance at two different banks in Luxembourg, and since it is such a small town our paths eventually crossed; he is 100-percent French with a thick accent. We are both highly organized and share many of the same goals in life. When I learned that Vincent was also interested in starting a business, I told him about Monsieur Palix and he was anxious to meet him. My father arranged it and we all really hit it off. He was happy to teach us and we were eager to learn!

We traveled around France with him for the next year to master this art, which is a very special caramel-making process. The more we learned, the more passionate we became about caramel and the careful craftsmanship that is required to make this flavorful mixture. 2009 was a big year for us: We started our factory, Le Caramel, and at the same time decided we were going to move "across the pond" to San Diego, California. It was also during this time that I was pregnant with our first son. We purchased the machines we needed to get up and running and actually shipped them over from France because they were the machines we learned on. We never looked back.

Trying to juggle everything can sometimes be a little difficult, but we manage because we are both very devoted to each other and our two young kids, as well as our business.

When my son, Martin, was a baby, we had a playpen in the office at the candy factory for him because we didn't have money for daycare. By the time my daughter, Caroline, came along, we had grown so much that there wasn't enough room for them to be in the office anymore. They are literally growing up in this business and enjoy it as much as we do.

In 2012 we made 180 tons of caramel; we are hoping to make 200 tons this year and it looks like we will easily hit that mark. We also create our candies and creams, and are looking to go into the industrial market with our syrup. We're working on developing new caramel products like caramel bits, which are yummy, crunchy caramel pieces you can put on top of ice cream or even cake icing. Our goal is to try and cover every single caramel need. We are so lucky to be able to make caramel every day and we absolutely love it!

END

# MARIAN RIVKIND

**M**arian Rivkind, a Toronto native, studied business management and creative advertising, and she worked for some of the largest and most prestigious advertising agencies in both Toronto, Canada, and London, England. She launched Yölka Chocolates in November of 2011, and continues to expand the luxurious line of confections, which have been featured in *O, The Oprah Magazine* (twice), Everyday with Rachael Ray, the *San Francisco Chronicle*, *Southern Living* magazine, and many more.

As a little girl living in Toronto, Canada, the holidays were a joyous but confusing time for my family. Born to Russian-Jewish parents but raised in a communist country, my parents had little knowledge of Jewish traditions and had adopted Russian holiday traditions instead. Upon leaving the old country to make a life in Canada, my mother stowed away precious, antique Russian glass ornaments. Every year around the holidays, my mother would take out these antique ornaments that resembled the 15th-century St. Basil's Cathedral with its colorful, ornate towers. We would then gather as a family and decorate our Yolka (Russian translation: "holiday tree").

1. Setting up my business was all about connecting the dots. First I researched what was currently being sold in the chocolate ornament department. Once I realized that there was a huge potential for what I was envisioning, I began the task of producing them myself using various-sized molds.

2. We started working on getting the chocolate sourced from a company that had the capabilities to produce on a large scale using the finest chocolate possible.

3. Once I found vendors to cover all aspects of the finished product, I had prototypes made. We worked on branding, package design, and the whole look and feel for what we wanted the brand to communicate.

4. Once we honed in on a brand personality, we took the product to the New York Gift Show where we found that our target audience (buyers) was completely receptive.

5. When the celebrity endorsements started coming in (Oprah!), we knew we had something really good.

FAVORITE QUOTE

"Look closely at the present you are constructing.
It should look like the future you are dreaming."
– Alice Walker

As my sister and I grew older, our interest in decorating the tree with these precious pieces became more appealing, much to my mother's dismay. These ornaments had survived a trip to the new world, but my mother knew they wouldn't survive the good intentions of our little fingers. We drew on our Russian heritage where families hung fruit and candy on trees as precious treats for the children of the house. My mother would wrap chocolate treats in tin foil and tie gold strings around the necks so my sister and I would be able to decorate our Yolka and at the same time be distracted from the precious glass. My fondest and most vivid memories are of the evenings around the holidays when we would get to pluck and unwrap the chocolates from the tree.

Fast-forward 20 years. My 4-year-old son begged to hang a treasured glass ornament; predictably, it fell and shattered. My first response was to recall my own childhood experience of my mother's creative holiday tradition, which I had long forgotten until that moment. I searched everywhere for these chocolate ornaments, but to no avail. Thus, the idea for Yölka was born. Today, my children continue to unwrap the tradition.

The business idea unraveled itself and made room in my life to explore and expand. Every direction I turned in this entrepreneurial venture lent itself to further development. It was as if every person I turned to had a tool to help me get further along. Never once was I road-blocked, discouraged, or defeated. A solution to whatever problem I had presented itself before I had time to question myself. It always felt right. I did my due diligence by creating the business plan, SWOT analysis, and everything else you're supposed to do before you invest in a business idea.

I knew all along I had something special, and that is worth cultivating and taking risks over. The most valuable thing I was told by a mentor in the beginning of my journey with Yölka was that 99 percent of the people around us are too afraid of taking a risk on what they believe would be a good business venture, and all you need to succeed is taking that risk. The success doesn't necessarily manifest in the way you had predicted it would, but it comes to you nonetheless in ways you could not have conceived.

**END**

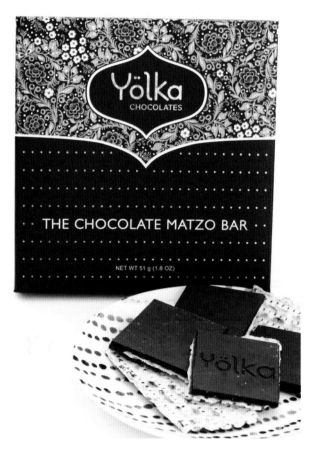

# PEGGY SHANNON

Queen City Cookies in Cincinnati was founded in 2010 by Peggy Shannon as a vehicle for her philanthropic vision to impact the world. A long-term supporter of social service and arts organizations, Peggy created the Queen City Cookies Art Camp, which provides free art activities to underserved children and supports conservation and animal rescue groups like The Orphan Project by the David Sheldrick Wildlife Trust, dedicated to fostering baby elephants, many orphaned by poachers. Queen City Cookies are unique pieces of edible art, handmade with love. These artisanal cookies are made from scratch using premium, natural ingredients, like rich, European-style butter, farm-fresh eggs, cane sugar, and unbleached flour. Sheer beauty to behold and bliss to taste!

I just celebrated my 55th birthday, which was very exciting because I feel like I'm coming into the prime of my life. I chose to celebrate it in a very adventurous and empowering way, looking forward to all that lies ahead. I have baked my entire life and love it; I even won at the state fair as a kid in 4-H for my pound cake.

When Mrs. Fields was just coming into our popular culture as an option for buying gourmet cookies, she came out with white chocolate macadamia cookies that blew my mind! I had started making uniquely flavored biscotti, getting back into baking and also providing myself with something sugar free. One day I went to get my mail, and on top of the stack was the Christmas 2008 issue of *Martha Stewart Living* and the cover featured these mesmerizing cookies. I had never seen anything so beautiful and elaborate; it was beyond my conception that you could produce a baked good that looked like that. It really stopped me in my tracks.

Later that day I was in the store Sur La Table and I saw some beautiful cookie molds, and I wondered if that's how they'd created those cookies on the cover. I bought one of the molds and on the back of it was the name of the manufacturer. I immediately went to their website and saw 800 different molds — my head exploded! My first order was for 13, the next week I ordered 25 more, and an addiction was born — today I have over 560 molds. I began making cookies using these amazingly detailed molds, and I shared them with family and friends who kept encouraging me to go into business.

I've really run the gamut on experience professionally and personally, everything from living in an ashram in Virginia at Yoga Ville to working at one of the United States' oldest, most prestigious law firms. I feel it is extremely important to be open and to try new things regardless of where those passions lie.

A few years ago when the economy had totally tanked, the city counsel of Cincinnati hadn't been able to balance our budget; as a result, the swimming pools were going to remain closed for the season. A very well-known philanthropist in town stepped up to the plate and underwrote the pools for the summer. I thought to myself, "This is just crazy that as a society we can't keep the pools open for kids … what's going on here!?" It pushed me over the edge. I knew we didn't really need another cookie company in this world, but I felt we needed a company that would use its efforts to fund organizations that needed support. I decided in that moment I was going to start a business and would dedicate our efforts to making a difference in our community.

In 2009 I started Queen City Cookies in my basement. After experiencing a little bit of success at Christmas I felt encouraged, so we quickly expanded to a carriage house that was on my property by converting it into a commercial kitchen.

FAVORITE QUOTE

"Let the beauty we love be what we do."
– Rumi

We also have our Schnecken ("snail" in German), which is like a sweet cinnamon roll on steroids. It's a traditional Jewish loaf, which came to Cincinnati long ago and has become a favorite in our region. It is baked in a loaf pan, and is an inverted sweet dough that is loaded with sugar and cinnamon and raisins. You roll the dough into a long spiral and then cut it into slices. We are the first in the country to make all of the different flavors. I was the first one to put bacon in our Schnecken and that was the runner up for outstanding new product of the year! You can't even believe how good it is! Some of our other flavors are chocolate bacon, apple bourbon pecan, and pumpkin marshmallow cream with roasted marshmallows on top. I am also working on a bourbon bacon because of the big bourbon craze and even a blueberry vanilla that will stop you in your tracks!

For our cookies, we are also designing new cookie boxes; each flavor has its own elephant design, and on the lid is a short story written in the voice of that particular elephant.

We've been very successful and have won a lot of awards, including a Sofi Award for 2nd place, Outstanding New Cookie of the Year, and Outstanding New Product of the Year, which catapulted us to a new level. In 2012 we bought a campus that consists of a historic church built in 1850; next to it is a rectory that now houses our offices on the second floor, and we turned the gymnasium into our wholesale bakery. We have a small retail shop and hope to create a high-end dessert bar on the first floor — that's the trajectory we are on. This business has its challenges, but it also brings a tremendous amount of creative excitement. It's really a lot of fun to get our product out there and support our organizations and community at the same time.

END

# KAT TAYLOR

Easy-going, fun-loving Kat Taylor does it all — she cooks, dish washer, waitress, and co-owner (along with her brother) of Nora's Fish Creek Inn located in Wilson, Wyoming. She works hard and plays harder. Their restaurant won the coveted James Beard Award in 2012. Nora's serves up real, down-home cooking, including their world-famous Huevos Rancheros, Trout & Eggs, and Sourdough Whole Wheat Banana Bread French Toast. If you are ever passing through, make sure Nora's is on your "must visit" list. You can't miss it — just look for the 20-foot trout on the roof!

My mother started the restaurant 32 years ago in 1981 and ran it very successfully. When she became ill, my brother and I took over. We are now buying the place from her so that she can finally slow down and enjoy life outside of the restaurant. Nora's has always been my mom's vision; without her, it would have never come into being. She taught me her recipes and how to cook. I am the muscle, and Trace, my brother, is the brain. I cook on the line, do all the baking, wash dishes, and my favorite thing … waitress. I love interacting with people and seeing the smiles when they try our food for the first time.

I didn't go to college, and now I understand why you should go to college!

"Unless you change how you are, you will always have what you've got."
– Jim Rohn

I'm not so good at the day-to-day business end of things, like getting back to people or answering emails. I used to get out of school early to come in and waitress for my mom, so now I have actually been here longer than she was.

At one point, having worked for my mom for quite awhile, I decided to try something different. I moved out to Pebble Beach, California, and went to work on a ranch as a ranch hand — you know, riding horses, cleaning out stalls, and that sort of thing. My brother, Trace, on the other hand, went to school and got a degree in engineering. Trace wasn't really interested in the restaurant business; although he would occasionally come in and run the night shift and tend bar. It's something that just kind of happened to him, but he was good at it.

The business end is the stressful part for me — that's where Trace steps up. I enjoy the creative aspect of what we do, inventing new recipes like my Sourdough Banana Bread French Toast, which has been a huge hit, or the Asparagus and Brie Omelette. I am trying to get in shape and lose a few pounds, so I created the Tomato, Basil, and Egg White Omelettes as a low-calorie option. Our lunch menu is broadening as well; everyone really loves the fish tacos we recently added. David Letterman and Harrison Ford both love our pancakes and have had several conversations on the air about them ... isn't that cool? We pride ourselves on serving the best breakfast in the Jackson Hole area.

Right now I am working on a new project: I have been canning our heavenly green chili salsa for a few years and selling it across the street at a little store called Hungry Jack's; I would like to see Nora's Green Chili Salsa selling in Smith's Grocery and Whole Foods stores nationwide. I am a people person and that's what I really love; after all, this is such a people-oriented business. I am learning how to better allocate duties to those who can do them best. I've found that nothing is as valuable to a business such as ours as being able to communicate properly with the people around you. Being unified is a very powerful thing. I am focused on learning all I can, business or otherwise. I want to eventually finish my house and continue to rodeo with my daughter. I plan on having a lot more fun in life!

**END**

# REBECCA WILLIAMS

Rebecca Williams is one of the remaining Atlanta natives. After years of living in other cities, she decided to come back home and grow where she was planted. She and her husband, Ross, co-own and operate Many Fold Farm, a 101-acre sheep dairy where they make hand-crafted cheeses, raise laying hens, and take care of a handful of very happy pigs!

I didn't know I wanted to be a farmer. I didn't really know what I wanted to do with my life except that I wanted to do something real and meaningful that did not take me away from my family — farming, as it turned out, completely fit the bill. My husband and I both love to take care of the land, animals, and people, and we share a core belief that these three things work together to serve and nourish each other.

FAVORITE QUOTE

"Ever tried, ever failed, no matter; try again, fail again, fail better."
– Samuel Beckett

Together, we worked at a number of farms on the East Coast, and we took advantage of whatever agricultural education we could find along the way. After a few years, we pooled our resources and bought a farm 30 miles from where we grew up along with two tickets to Burlington, Vermont, to study at the Vermont Institute for Artisan Cheese.

I am now the head cheesemaker, head of marketing, head of personnel and hiring, part-time farm hand, assistant sheep midwife, customer relations manager, chief logistics operator, part-time egg packer, and CEO of our farm. The journey to this point has been anything but straightforward. The learning curve has been steep and, more often than not, the pattern of two steps forward, one step back has prevailed.

Every day on the farm is an exercise in embracing failure. Every day something goes wrong, something needs fixing, or some unexpected hurdle is suddenly in front of us. We are not commonly taught that failure is the essential feature of success. No one undertakes a successful project without coping with frequent failures. It is my advice to anyone starting their own business to think very carefully about how they react when they fail, especially when it's the little things that are failing. It will tell you a lot about how your business might fare in the long term, and how your business fares will tell you an awful lot about who you are.

**END**

## Farm Facts:

1. There are 101 acres on the farm, about 10 people work here, and we have 200 sheep, 3 dogs, and 400 chickens.

2. Our products stem from the belief that healthy land makes healthy animals makes healthy people.

3. We offer a variety of farmstead cheeses made right here on the farm from the milk of our own ewes.

4. Our eggs are from hens raised on pasture; the yolks are bright orange, packed with vitamins and minerals (from all the grass and grubs the hens eat that factory chickens never get), and they are unlike anything you would find at the supermarket, even the organic free-range eggs.

5. Our lambs are born and raised here on the farm, and they eat nothing but mother's milk and fresh green grass (fertilized by chickens, not chemicals).

6. Our sheep are sheared once a year in late winter. We ship the wool to a woolen mill north of Calgary, Canada, for cleaning and carding, and it comes back to us as beautiful two-ply yarn and fluffy roving for hand spinning.

7. All of our products are grown and raised on our farm using a grass-based system. This means that grass is either the sole or the primary food all the animals on our farm consume. We implement a management-intensive rotational grazing strategy that directly mimics the development of grasslands in nature, providing us with maximum soil fertility, maximum grass growth, and maximum nutrition for our animals and our customers.

# JOY WILSON

Los Angeles-based Joy Wilson is the new super girl wonder in the world of baking —she's sweet as dessert with a little bit of an edge. Her tremendously popular blog is all a twitter with funky, creative culinary excitement and has been named one of the Top 50 Food Blogs in the World by the *London Times*. *Saveur* named Joy the Baker the Best Baking and Dessert Blog of 2011, and Foodbuzz, Forbes, and *Food and Wine* magazine have all followed suit with high praise. Her distinctive style with food, photography, and words combines to create pure magic in the kitchen.

I run a food blog called Joy the Baker, which has been up and running since 2008. I'm a trained baker, so I bake things, write about it, and take pictures of the food I make. It's sort of a compulsion — it's my absolute passion and I am obsessed with all things delicious. My love of baking came from my dad. He taught me at a very young age while I literally grew up in the kitchen. He's not a professional, but he's an extremely enthusiastic home baker, and he instilled in me a great love of cookies and pie!

## 3 Tips on Blogging:

1. Go at your own pace! You're the boss of you. Set a loose posting schedule that works for you and try hard to reach those goals. Push yourself, but be kind to yourself — both feel really good.

2. Don't pay any mind to Internet rankings. Do what you do, and keep doing it better and better. Be your own barometer.

3. Support is a big part of the blogging community. Reading other people's work, admiring photography, re-pinning, re-tweeting, liking, commenting, high-fiving — it's all part of the support game. So ... let's support each other!

"The biggest adventure you can take is to live the life of your dreams."
– Oprah Winfrey

My first job was in the food industry, dipping ice cream for Ben & Jerry's, and truly everything blossomed from there. About five years ago I was fired from a baking job, which felt very traumatic at the time. I really needed to find a creative outlet for all the baking that I still wanted to do. It wasn't like I had anything planned: I started taking pictures of the food I made at home with my little camera phone (nothing fancy, but it got the job done), and posting them online with stories about my life and my current circumstances. I think I was mostly looking for a place to share my recipes, not knowing what that would look like or even what it could turn into. Suddenly, a lot of people were visiting my blog and commenting, and that's how this whole thing got started.

During the first three years of my blog, I had a couple of part-time jobs as well. I would get up in the morning and go to work, come home for a while, and then go to my evening job at a local restaurant. When I got off at midnight all my friends would go out for cocktails and I'd go home and work on a blog post. But you know what? It felt awesome!

My first cookbook was released in 2012 by Hyperion; it's called "Joy the Baker Cookbook: 100 Simple and Comforting Recipes." I try to make my food very approachable for the home cook. I want you to feel like you can get in the kitchen and come out with something delicious that you can be really proud of, something you'd want to take to a party. I'm now hard at work on my second cookbook, which is totally exciting and a dream come true, times two! I want this one to feel a bit more grown up with some indulgent, classy recipes — something that might be a stretch for the home cook — but it will be presented in a way that makes people want to reach and learn new skills in their kitchen. Look for it sometime in 2014.

I'm still going strong with the blog and have been co-developing a weekly Joy the Baker podcast at homefries.com, which offers a candid look behind the scenes. On the podcast, my friend, Tracy Benjamin, and I talk about recipes, photography, and life in general; it's silly and funny, but informative too. I'm also working on a web video series that I will be hosting called "We're About to Be Friends," which is also at homefries. com. Each episode will feature personalities from my favorite websites, cooking shows, and best-selling cookbook authors; lessons will be learned, secrets will be revealed, and hopefully friends will be made. And even further on the horizon are plans for a third cookbook!

Around the time I started all of this, I heard Oprah say that if you follow the thing you love the most, you'll be successful. At the time I understood this superficially, but I didn't know what the manifestation of that could really be — I feel like I get it now. What Oprah doesn't tell you is that it's a tremendous amount of hard work, and it can be scary doing the thing you love and making a living from it. It's also really exciting, rewarding, and super fun almost every day, if you are brave enough to keep at it. All in all, it's an incredibly sweet life!

**END**

# PAIGE WITHERINGTON

Paige Witherington is a Southern girl, born and raised in Germantown, Tennessee. At the age of 20, she found her passion working in the soil and with beautiful produce. After graduating with a biosystems engineering degree from Clemson, she pursued her future career apprenticing at a farm in the Hudson Valley of New York. Two years later she landed at Serenbe Farms to manage the sustainable vegetable farming operation. At 31, she's been farming for over 10 years and managing Serenbe Farms for almost 8 years, learning more from the land and Mother Nature every year. Today, Paige manages the farm with her fiancé, Justin Dansby.

My journey to becoming a successful organic farmer was inspired by good food, nature, problem solving, and hard work.

I had a fairly distant relationship with good food growing up. My favorite meal was the familiar blue box of macaroni and cheese with frozen chicken tenders. As a kid, potatoes were the vegetable in my diet. While I was a very picky eater, I did get to enjoy some good Southern food on my grandparents' tables, but didn't value the small gardens they'd tend in their backyards or their pantries full of homegrown, canned goods. My first farm experience allowed me to harvest lettuce greens and construct the freshest, most delicious salad that I'd ever tasted. Now, growing year round, we never have to purchase any vegetables and our plates are always vibrant, healthy, organic, and fresh from our farm.

"We all have dreams. But in order to make dreams come into reality, it takes an awful lot of determination, dedication, self-discipline, and effort."
—Jesse Owen

My fondness of nature and being outside emerged as a kid. Even growing up in suburbia, I sought outdoor experiences and pursued many hobbies that had me surrounded by nature. Mother Nature is so complex, and each year we learn more and more from the land. At Serenbe Farms our organic matter and soil health was almost non-existent due to the erosive and poor farming practices of prior years. Each year we amend, balance, and add back to our soils, restoring our patch of life that gives us thousands of pounds of produce each year. Last year alone we harvested over 80,000 pounds of produce!

I always excelled in math and science, and I am constantly utilizing my engineering education. I take pleasure in figuring out solutions to complex problems and thinking on my toes. Part of what I love about farming is the balance of brain and brawn.

Coming up with the farm list and orchestrating our farm crew, harvest times, and planting schedules within the constraints of temperature, weather, and efficiency of movement can be like figuring out a giant puzzle. One of my favorite parts of this job is simplifying, organizing, and making sure that we work purposefully and intentionally. Our end goals are to nourish the land, serve beautiful and fresh produce to our customers, teach others about farming, and create community through food. The intellectual balance of farming also allows us to be good teachers. On our farm, we've helped grow over a dozen farmers through our apprenticeship program. Another problem to solve is that of economics and keeping the farm profitable, which requires management skills that I hadn't learned in school; it takes a willingness to listen to feedback, take risks, and keep good records.

I have been dedicated to running and athletics since I was a child. Within these sports, hard work became synonymous with success. Without the time, will, and effort put into training or racing, it would be difficult to progress. From these life experiences, I have become very fond of hard and punishing work. Farming is not often easy; it requires observation, time, strength, and an incredible desire to see an end result. Fatigue and stress come with our long, hot summers and our heavy harvests, but persistence and dedication help us to push through so that we can enjoy feeding our local families and feeling good about what we're doing for the land and the health of our community.

Finding a job that encompasses my values in life keeps me happy and passionate about what I do and in turn keeps my farm business successful. I find that happiness and profit within a business follow passion. Without passion, it'd be hard to succeed.

END

## Farm Facts:

1. Serenbe Farms is a certified-organic sustainable farm southwest of Atlanta, Georgia.

2. The farm is 25 acres and there are currently five people who work on it.

3. The farm offers over 350 varieties of vegetables, herbs, flowers, fruits, and mushrooms. Their produce is distributed within 40 miles of the farm through their own CSA (Community Supported Agriculture) program, Serenbe Farmers, Artists Markets, and local restaurants.

4. At Serenbe Farms we live by three organic methods: composting, cover cropping, and crop rotation ... the three C's. Our compost is made using a combination of food waste from Serenbe residents, restaurants, and plant materials.

5. Cover cropping is the practice of growing rich green grasses and legumes to create organic matter to incorporate back into the soil. In addition to nutrition, cover crops help alleviate erosion, reduce weeds, break pest and disease cycles, attract wildlife, and are very pretty.

6. We employ a 10-year crop rotation; this ensures the disruption of disease and pest cycles and ensures that we aren't depleting the same nutrients year after year.